Praise for
Going Forward:
Downsizing, Moving and Settling In
By Moreen Torpy

Going Forward: Downsizing, Moving and Settling In is an excellent resource. The book starts with an illuminating review of the reasons, emotions and excuses we have around all the stuff we keep. With humor and compassion, Moreen Torpy encourages us to let go, or to help others let go, and then gets into the practical details. She includes lots of step by step advice, excellent references if more information is needed on a topic, and downloadable worksheets to help you organize your own or another's move. In addition, this book offers advice on helping seniors to move that is both sensitive and sensible. Highly recommended for those thinking of perhaps downsizing themselves or faced with the necessity of helping and older friend or relative to move.

Morva Bowman, MBA
Masters of Space and Time

Moreen Torpy's book, *Going Forward: Downsizing, Moving and Settling In* takes you through all the steps in the moving process. By taking the time to complete the worksheets and exercises, you will be certainly be able to take the right steps to reduce the stress of your move.

Interesting and thought-provoking anecdotes, quotes and illustrations make this book a handy resource for people on the move!

Karen Shinn, CPCA
Downsizing Diva
Co-Author of *GO! The Essential Guide to Organizing and Moving*

This is such a helpful resource, for anyone who is thinking of moving. Using the tools in this book will definitely prepare you for downsizing, moving and settling in. Implementing the strategies suggested in *Going Forward: Downsizing, Moving and Settling In* will eliminate the stress and in turn organize your move.

Brenda Scagnetti Clement
Senior Relocation Specialist
Complete Organizational Services LLC

Whether it is simplifying our lives or setting priorities, Moreen's down-to-earth approach is refreshing. She offers timely advice given the financial crisis faced by many and the ever aging population. Emotionally charged decisions are treated with sensitivity, empathy, and gentleness while showing how to embracing a new stage in life. Her suggestions and worksheets address all needs of the people experiencing the downsizing, not just the "stuff" being moved. Everyone will experience downsizing at some point in their lives and *Going Forward: Downsizing, Moving and Settling In* will certainly become a favorite guide.

Brenda Wiltshire
Mirror Images Life Coach

If you are contemplating a move or are helping someone else with a move then this easy to read book will be a helpful tool for the journey ahead.

Moreen is bang on with her information. I love this statement Moreen shared...it is so true, *If you look back, you'll probably note that this is a lifetime of accumulation so it can't be purged overnight.*

Going Forward: Downsizing, Moving and Settling In is a well written, comprehensive easy to follow manual for helping you with a major life transition.

Elaine Shannon
Empress of Inspiration, Professional Organizer
Award winning video producer (Organizing Connection)

Moreen Torpy touches on something very powerful here. It's not really about downsizing at all, but more about "right sizing." Having just "right sized" myself, I understand the mental shift, the commitment, and the planning that is involved. I also know the FREEDOM that comes from being on the other side. Moreen captures everything in this book to help you move through the process with support. You will experience a magical journey if you choose to see this as a gift, not only for yourself but your family as well.

Marlo Nikkila
Life Coach and former Professional Organizer

Moreen has written a very practical, compassionate guide to help people through the process of downsizing. It is especially helpful that she has included tips for the whole series of events, from planning tips to living their new smaller-space lifestyle.

I love Moreen's practical, compassionate guide. She guides readers through the downsizing process with humor and common sense.

Laurene Livesey Park, CPO-CD®
Professional Organizer, Speaker, Author
OrganizeMe101.com

Moving Forward: Downsizing, Moving and Settling In is written by a Professional Organizer with obvious experience in the very real and intricate personal issues that come with downsizing and moving seniors. A book recommended for family and friends of those *Moving Forward*. In fact, most looking forward baby boomers will be able to find some wisdom pertinent to their own future. As a Professional Organizer, I also appreciated the many tips for helping people sift through the challenges of their stuff, and make peace with their past. Enjoy the read, then call your local Professional Organizer for help!

Elinor Warkentin
Goodbye Clutter! Consulting and Organizing Services

As a professional organizer and senior move manager, I found *Going Forward: Downsizing, Moving and Settling In* insightful and instructive. I especially liked the section on Packing for a Senior. There are so many helpful pointers that a person who is downsizing and/or moving will find invaluable. The information in this book makes it a definite keeper.

Brenden McDaniel CPO-CD, cSMM
Co Author of *The ICD Guide to Challenging Disorganization: For Professional Organizers*
Action Organizing Services LLC

In this easy-to-read book, fellow professional organizer Moreen simplifies what downsizing is all about. She includes clear, helpful tips and worksheets. Moreen with her down-to-earth, friendly manner illustrates real-life examples that often occur when downsizing. Whether you're right-sizing for yourself or helping a family member downsize, this book will provide the guidance you need.

Jacki Hollywood Brown
Organizing and Productivity Consultant
J-organize

Also by Moreen Torpy:

Let's Get Organized: 172 Tiplets to Simplify Life

Christmas Workbook: how to plan and create a more meaningful Christmas

GOING FORWARD:
Downsizing, Moving and Settling In

MOREEN TORPY

Editor: Mark Sandford
Illustrator: Marcello Pettella

BALBOA
PRESS

A DIVISION OF HAY HOUSE

This book is intended for education and discussion purposes only. For legal advice, please consult a lawyer.

Names and details of the case studies have been changed to ensure confidentiality.

Balboa Press books may be ordered through booksellers or by contacting:

Balboa Press
A Division of Hay House
1663 Liberty Drive
Bloomington, IN 47403
www.balboapress.com
1-(877) 407-4847

ISBN: 978-1-4525-4514-1 (sc)
ISBN: 978-1-4525-4515-8 (e)

Library of Congress Control Number: 2011963739

The author of this book does not dispense medical advice or prescribe the use of any technique as a form of treatment for physical, emotional, or medical problems without the advice of a physician, either directly or indirectly. The intent of the author is only to offer information of a general nature to help you in your quest for emotional and spiritual well-being. In the event you use any of the information in this book for yourself, which is your constitutional right, the author and the publisher assume no responsibility for your actions.

Printed in the United States of America

Balboa Press rev. date: 3/21/2012

To my clients, past, present and future.

CONTENTS

INTRODUCTION

What an odd word 'downsize'. It first appeared in the Merriam-Webster Dictionary in 1975. It's a verb meaning, for our purposes, *to reduce in size, especially to design or produce in smaller size.*[1] It's also a lifestyle choice: What's more important, our belongings or the people in our lives?

I have downsized and moved a number of times, most recently into a condo from a house. The process has been both surprising and difficult. Surprising to learn how much stuff I really had, and how difficult it is to let go of what needs to go so my new home is comfortable and not a storage facility.

We will discuss downsizing from the perspective of reducing the size of our living quarters and the number of objects we own. By reducing our material belongings we create more room in life to grow without being encumbered by them.

I believe that if we haven't grown in our lives, we haven't really lived. Personal growth sometimes takes unhappy turns, but it is growth nevertheless and we can embrace it to create a happier future. Sometimes in order to grow, we need to divest ourselves of material goods.

I DOWNSIZING

"You cannot solve a problem until you acknowledge that you have one and accept responsibility for solving it."
~ Zig Ziglar (Author, Motivational Speaker)

This doesn't have to be a negative, nor is it a step backward, but a step toward the future. The term 'right-sizing' could easily be used instead. A home that was right 20 years ago when five or six people lived in it may be too large now with only one or two still there. Life has changed and the time has arrived to make some decisions. Once you get going, you may wonder why it took so long.

At first, you may feel some sadness letting go of household items you took years to accumulate. But that's quite normal. Allow yourself time to feel this and talk about it with a trusted friend.

On the other hand, this may be the beginning of a new life that has been in the back of your mind for some time, a happier more carefree life you can't wait to start.

Living in a smaller place doesn't mean living without style. There are plenty of ways to live large in a small space. It's all about attitude, creativity, storage and decorating.

In today's world, with the so-called economic crisis bearing down, downsizing can take quite a different trajectory.

Foreclosures of homes bought with funds the purchaser did not have, or was unable to obtain, has added a different dimension to our downsizing story. The dream for the biggest McMansion on the street needs to be revised, or maybe just postponed.

Ask yourself what you're sacrificing in order to have this big house. Is it sleep? Is your health suffering? Is it time with your family? Or is it your financial ability to pay for your children's education?

It's quite alright to change a dream, change direction, to decide that what you now have isn't sustainable and let it all go in order to achieve peace in your life, knowing you can deal with the curves life may throw at you.

1. A Life Stage

We spend the first part of our adult lives collecting the items we need to live independently. It's almost a rite of passage from life as a student to life as a self-supporting adult. Our needs change. We need business clothes, so we purchase them with the money we're now earning. We might move into our own apartment and need furniture for it. Then we collect artwork we like, and so it goes.

After some time, our tastes may change, so we change our look—both our wardrobe and décor. This may happen a few more times throughout our adult lives.

Then comes a time when we realize we don't need any more stuff. Our values have changed direction. We begin to rethink all the items we've acquired over the years and wonder why we have so much. We begin thinking about changing our lifestyle and letting go of some of this.

We might be approaching retirement age and decide we have everything we need, and possibly more.

With changing values, owning a lot of material goods might not fit.

"Be content with what you have,
rejoice in the way things are.
When you realize there is nothing lacking,
the whole world belongs to you."
~ Lao Tzu (6th Century BC philosopher)

Why Downsize?

There are as many reasons as there are individuals who are going through the exercise. Here are a few:

- Lifestyle shift
- Smaller carbon footprint
- Smaller place
- Moving cross-country or overseas
- Change in family (divorce, death, empty nest)
- Retirement
- Economics
- Move to adult community
- To be closer to family
- Health
- To be closer to health-care facilities
- Reduce utilities cost
- Simplify life
- Minimize monthly expenses

Downsizing does not necessarily mean a move to smaller living quarters. We might simply realize we have more stuff than our home can comfortably house. Sometimes it's advantageous to pretend we're moving as a motivator to edit whatever is not absolutely necessary to our daily lives.

The best part of downsizing your life--happiness arrives by your experiencing a life that matters on a deeper level now and in the future.

We can talk about downsizing our commitments, as well. When they get out of hand, we have no time for the priorities in life.

Simplify

"The ability to simplify means to eliminate the unnecessary so that the necessary may speak."
~ Hans Hoffman (1880-1966, German Painter)

Have you noticed that on vacation you can do with much less? Less clothing, fewer household conveniences (think rustic cottage, boat or trailer/RV). If we're travelling for business, we may look for a hotel with a coffee maker and hair dryer in our room, but the other amenities don't matter so much. When we visit friends for a period of time, we take with us only the barest necessities. We can live with less sometimes—why not all the time? We would definitely spend less time on housework and other maintenance projects. On vacation, we're also away from all the commitments that keep us busy. How many of them are really that important to the big picture?

Priorities

What's the most important thing in your life? The fastest and easiest way to find out is to look at your checkbook, bank statement, credit card statement and calendar. Where your money and time go indicate what your priorities are. If what you see doesn't match what you believe your real priorities to be, you may wish to change a few things.

Below is a worksheet to help you get started. (For full sized worksheets, go to www.goforwarddownsize.com/specialgift.) Using the documents noted above, fill out the table with the information you have. Study the priorities as they are and how you've been dealing with them. Then decide what needs to be changed, if anything, and re-prioritize according to what you believe your priorities need to be in the future. Be honest with yourself so this will work.

Seeing this in black and white will give you a good start on how to begin downsizing.

Priorities worksheet:

	CURRENT PRIORITY	How do I deal with this	Changes needed	RE-PRIORITIZE
1	E.g. Wardrobe must always be in fashion.	Buy new clothes every season.	Learn to wear clothes for more than one season.	Save for retirement.
2				
3				

Times Change

We might begin to think all that stuff takes more maintenance than it's worth. We're worried something could happen to it. Apart from the usual concerns like fire or theft, we may be thinking about changing technology. We notice our cassette deck doesn't work any more. There's nowhere to have it fixed or purchase a new tape player because the technology is obsolete. So we must decide whether to live without the music or invest in a CD or MP3 player and replace each tape.

We might be thinking about moving into a smaller home now that the nest is empty. Or we just want a smaller home to benefit from the advantages of one. What will we do with all the furniture? At one time, people didn't need to worry about that because everything was handed down to the next generation. Today, the next generation is less interested in their parents' treasures—fine china, furniture, crystal and silver that needs polishing. If it doesn't go into the dishwasher, many don't want it.

Maybe we're dealing with a merged household and all the associated material goods. What do we keep and what do we let go? The decisions can be difficult and take years to implement.

The concept of *bigger, better, more* is beginning to wear thin. Often the reverse is true, and we notice our values changing. We begin to believe that less is more and buying quality is better than quantity.

Values

Values are much like priorities. Where our money and time go indicate our current values. Using the table below, write your values as indicated by your schedule, and other ways you spend your time. Study these and make changes accordingly.

How does this help with downsizing? Simple. If we're spending all our time maintaining a large home or collections of memorabilia, or going to unproductive meetings, perhaps a re-evaluation would be useful.

"You'll always pay a price when you choose to keep a thing: The time, money, or energy needed to house and maintain it."
~ Cindy Glovinsky, M.S.W., A.C.S.W

Values worksheet:

	CURRENT VALUES	How do I deal with this	Changes needed	RE-EVALUATE
1	e.g. running the city soccer league	This comes first in my life.	Step back from the full responsibility	My time is more valuable to my family than to soccer
2				
3				

Smaller Home

1. Advantages

- Reduced heating and cooling bills in an apartment, condo or townhouse as we will benefit from the ambient heat, or air conditioning, of those above, beside and below us

- Less space to put purchases so we don't buy as much
- Less space so we develop closer relationships with our family
- More time for ourselves, family, travel, hobbies, or spent at the cottage or other holiday property
- Less maintenance
- Better cash flow
- Smaller carbon footprint

2. *Disadvantages*

- No guest room (possibly)
- Fewer opportunities to be alone if more than one person lives there
- Fewer belongings
- Less storage

Bust that Myth

I've heard many people say: "I don't need to deal with this yet. I'm not moving for a long time!" The reality, however, is that downsizing takes much longer than you think it will. Why? Possibly because you have a lot more than you think you have. Or maybe as you stroll down memory lane, the time flies by quickly. You might feel emotional going through your treasures and either take time away from the project or feel unable to continue. In light of this, I suggest you work with someone who will understand when you relive the memories, gently deal with the emotions and help you keep going.

If you've already applied for an independent apartment or to a retirement home, the space might become available sooner than you expect. In my experience, when this happens, you don't have much time to move in. It's sometimes only a day or two in the case of a retirement home or care facility. Beginning to downsize then will not allow you to complete the project in a few hours. Deciding what furniture will fit into the new place could take that long, without ever touching everything else.

Or you might suffer a medical crisis and not be able to make your own decisions. I'm sure you know of someone who fell, suffered a stroke, or some other debilitating incident, making it impossible for him or her to live alone. I don't want to be the bearer of bad news; however, this person could be you. Isn't it better to start now and decide yourself where your treasures go?

Never too soon

Think about your joy-to-stuff ratio. That's "the time a person has to enjoy life versus the time a person spends accumulating material goods."[1]

If you're not enjoying your things, let them go. And if there's not enough space for them, is there any question? Then don't acquire more. You haven't any more time to enjoy things than you did before letting the first batch go.

Are you thinking that it's important to make your own decisions about who gets what? Wouldn't it be easier to deal with that now while you can tell the stories that go along with each item?

"To ask how little, not how much, can I get along with.
To say 'is it necessary?' when I am tempted
to add one more accumulation to my lift."
~ Ann Morrow Lindbergh (1906-2001, Aviator)

Make weeding out before a move your lifestyle, eclipsing everything else if you've let stuff accumulate.

By starting early, you'll have plenty of time to share memories of the items you've collected. And you'll also have plenty of time to record the stories that go along with these important items. Whether you keep them or pass them on to the next generation, it's important to include the history. If the next generation doesn't know an item's history, certainly whomever they pass the item on to will not know it either.

Some experts say it will take six to 12 months to completely downsize and do it well. Like many projects, it could take much longer.

Another point: If you delay downsizing, everything ends up coming to your new home and will need to be dealt with there, in less space.

One example of this is Andy, an event planner with rooms full of decorations, who moved from a 3,000-square-foot home to a 1,200-square-foot apartment. A saver, he reported, "Our organizer told us 'you do not have to get rid of anything. You are not obligated to throw anything out.' Knowing that we could keep stuff was 'free-ing.' It made choosing easier and it made getting rid of stuff easier."

Downsizing another's collection:

Not long ago, the media reported the saga of a woman who moved from a four-bedroom, three-storey home with an attic, basement and garage to a two-bedroom apartment. In itself, that doesn't sound so interesting, but the real story was that her husband had been a packrat who frequented garage sales. It took her three months working daily to sort, give away, sell and toss to prepare for her move. She must have worked day and night to accomplish this. Moral: Allow plenty of time to downsize.

Are you living with the perceived responsibility of caring for family heirlooms? Are you asking yourself if and how to get rid of the ones you have no use or place for? By starting early, you can survey the family to be sure no one else wants these, and decide where they will go from your home.

If you are moving as a family, everyone needs to have a decision in the downsizing. Children can decide where their unused toys will go, and your partner will be able to tell you what's really important to him/her so it doesn't go out the door. Adult children can claim their childhood treasures, like the Barbie collection or toy trains. If they don't want the treasures you've saved for them, consider giving them to other family or friends, or donating them. You may be able to request an income tax receipt depending on the item and where it goes.

But it wasn't expensive

Just because something is inexpensive doesn't give it permission to occupy space in your home. Avoid dollar stores, yard sales and thrift stores.

Over the years, our worldly goods multiply. We don't realize it because we're busy living our lives. We continue purchasing items needed at the time (or maybe multiples if we can't find the originals), and when they outlive their value, they take up residence somewhere in our home where they're out of sight and eventually out of mind. Repeating this process increases the quantity of stuff we store under stairs, in the back of closets and in dark basements.

Clutter breeds clutter. Have you ever noticed that if one thing is left out of place, suddenly it's a pile? Clutter is a magnet. Scientists may not agree, but I've seen it happen.

Maybe collecting and saving was for a future that was sidetracked. Sue and Joel rescued children's furniture from their friends whose children had outgrown it in anticipation of their own children to come. Children never came for that couple, so they eventually gave away the furniture that had become clutter.

Are you keeping your children's toys for your grandchildren? Think about how legislation changes regarding safety, and whether these toys would make the cut. Or maybe your grandchildren will live across the world from you and never have an opportunity to play with these toys.

A lifetime of accumulation can't be purged overnight.

As soon as it goes, I'll need it

That's unlikely, and such an old wives' tale. So what if you do? You can borrow the item, purchase a new one or use something you already have in its place. For example, Josie could use a colander for draining pasta, but finds the inside of a salad spinner works just as well.

Ask yourself if it's truly a keepsake or simply junk. Be brutally honest with yourself.

But it's all good (or expensive). I can't just give it away!

Yes you can. If it's not useful, doesn't fit you or your lifestyle, or you don't absolutely love the item, you don't need it. Price is not a reason to keep something useless. Consider selling it on consignment if that helps you feel better. Then you can use that money to purchase something you really need and will enjoy using.

Real estate people tell me when they're listing a property for sale, they see that at least half of what's in the home is unnecessary and ask the homeowner to remove it before they show the house.

Great Aunt Betsie gave it to me. I have to keep it

Again, you're not obliged to keep anything you don't love and use regularly. Don't fall into the trap of feeling like the curator of all things family. Pass them on to another family member who will love and use them. If no one else wants it, pass it along to someone who does.

What about unwanted gifts? Re-gift them. It's quite acceptable today to do so. Just ensure you don't return the item to the person who gave it to you! To feel comfortable, you must separate the gift from the giver. It's not an extension of them that needs to be loved and cherished, except if the gift is something alive.

There are various ways to pass on gifts that don't suit you. Apart from re-gifting, you could also hold an "unwanted gift" brunch with friends where everyone brings something to exchange for something they prefer. Or you could throw a "giveaway party" where the guests take away something of yours and leave nothing.

If you feel awkward about this, don't do it. You could be up front with the giver and explain that the item doesn't work for you for a valid reason—it's too small, too large or you already have 18 just like it. Never make the giver feel you're not grateful for a gift.

How does clutter happen?

It begins in the mind, manifests in our life then takes over our space. When we're not able to think clearly, our physical surroundings show this. We tend to let organization slide and maybe even let the cleaning slide, as well. Before long, we're embarrassed to invite anyone in. Remember that one coat hung on a chair that suddenly became a pile? Continuous repetition of this behavior creates chaos—and clutter.

On the positive side, clutter can be a temporary state, for example, when moving, doing a major housecleaning or redecorating. Our homes are out of order due to the project at hand. Once this is completed, order returns.

Disorder can also be caused by medical or emotional issues. Grief can lead us to engage in retail therapy—buying lots of stuff to make us feel better. But after a short while, this good feeling wears off. Then we purchase more stuff. In the extreme, such behavior can eat all of our income and savings, with nothing but clutter to show for it—and an empty bank account or maxed-out credit cards.

Another time people might have things they don't need is when dementia occurs. We might forget we've bought something we need, and continue buying the same thing repeatedly. Andrea's actions are a case in point. When I was working with her, she had about a 10 years' supply of dishwashing liquid and had no idea what she had done.

Maybe we're a bit of a perfectionist. If we don't have time to do something perfectly, we put it off. That's when procrastination joins the party. They are two sides of the same coin; they feed on each other, and eventually clutter is the result. By breaking that cycle, we reverse this to a temporary situation. If we cannot break the cycle, the mess will continue to grow until it's out of hand.

The next time you're tempted to drop something "just for now," think again. Like that friendship cake starter, it could be the beginning of another pile of clutter.

If none of this resonates with you, consider whether you're building a wall of clutter to shield yourself from something. I suggest you think carefully about this and find a resolution.

Consumerism

Consumerism is another clutter culprit. Advertisers try to make us believe we need things we really don't. I call these artificial needs. Wants and needs get all mixed up. Ask "How much is enough?" Aldus Huxley, author of *1984* and *Brave New World,* said "to *consume* takes the masses' minds off the real issues." It's something to think about and it does relate to the retail therapy we discussed above.

Clients tell me they can't get organized because their house is too small—usually it's because they have far more stuff than they need. One situation that comes to mind concerns Lisa, a mom who continually buys children's videos at yard sales and discount stores for her little ones. When I met the family, there were more videos than the children could possibly view before reaching high school.

Then there are those yard sales and thrift stores calling to us to rescue what others have cast off. Don't fall for this.

2. Scaling Down

"We don't need to increase our goods nearly as much
as we need to scale down our wants.
Not wanting something is as good as possessing it."
~ Donald Horban

Stuff can be a heavy anchor that weighs us down, encumbers us. We are not our stuff. What we have doesn't bestow on us importance in the world. How sad if that's how we identify ourselves.

In her book *Peaceful Spaces*, Alice Whatley says, "By questioning the purpose of everything you own, you will quickly realize that it is you, rather than the stuff that surrounds you, that must take center stage in the home."[2]

Do you see your stuff as protection against homelessness? Is a cherished item a reminder of other times—youth, vibrant life? Is it a status symbol? Do you really need all of it in your daily life now? What if you experienced a serious event that caused a major life change? What would happen to this then?

People's relationships with stuff are complicated. There's no magic wand to make it go away. If there were, everyone would have one. If you can't remember why you've kept something, it's probably not worth keeping.

Downsizing and moving can be stressful. You're dealing with years of accumulation. And if you've lived in the same home for many years, multiply the stress accordingly.

And it's not only the collection of this world's goods. It's also the collection of memories you've created in this place. Moving is leaving some of them behind, as well.

If your home was on fire, what you would grab to save? (The fire department would say, 'Take nothing, just get out'.) Use the response to this to prioritize the importance of your belongings. What would you replace if your home burned to the ground? The rest probably isn't that important and not worth keeping.

Now is the best time to inventory what you have to see where you are today in order to determine where you'd rather be. That is how you'd prefer to spend your time and energy. It may be surprising to realize there's a difference between the two.

Consider this: Thomas Merton said: "We cannot use created things without anxiety unless we are detached from them."

The same applies to a large home. When the economy takes a downturn, can you still afford the mortgage? Or will the bank evict you? You might want to think about this and either offload the McMansion now or plan to do it as soon as you can—certainly before you have to learn to downsize the hard way.

It's interesting how families are smaller today than a few generations ago, yet the houses have grown to the point that sometimes they can be a millstone dragging us down. We don't want our dream home to become a nightmare!

Beware of identity theft

When sorting your papers, ensure nothing can be removed to steal your identity. This is one of the fastest-growing crimes today. Always shred paper with anything on it that someone could use to impersonate you and create financial grief for you.

Shred all bills, credit card slips and statements, bank statements, interact slips, and especially the unsolicited, pre-approved offers for credit cards. Definitely shred anything with your signature on it. Use a cross-cut shredder for additional security.

There are two types of downsizing—ourselves and others. Let's begin with downsizing ourselves. Now might be a good time to do some soul-searching about what your belongings really mean to you.

3. Downsizing Self

By downsizing our belongings, we create more freedom in many ways.

The first assignment when beginning to downsize is to record and analyze what downsizing means for you. Write the pros and cons in separate columns. When you've finished, the answers will be very clear.

You could use a chart like this. Simply add the number of lines you need.

Downsizing Self Worksheet:

PRO	CON
e.g. keeping up my place is too much for me now	I won't have space for my children when they come home to visit.

Why are you thinking of downsizing? Do you want to take the equity from selling your house? Is your nest empty and you don't need as much space? Do you want to move closer to family, in another city perhaps?

Maybe you're seeking more contentment and satisfaction in your living arrangements. Maybe it's time to shed what you no longer need or desire in life. Maybe you want to make space for your future to receive new, better and more desirable experiences or relationships. Maybe you just need a positive change in your life, for whatever reason.

Think about how your space looks now. Is it cluttered to the point that you're embarrassed to invite friends in? Is it saying you have difficulty concentrating or making decisions (can't decide where to put something, so the pile begins)? Is it saying you're trapped in the past (everything showing its age, not well maintained)?

It might be easier to downsize when you have some goals in mind. Perhaps you want to travel more to visit children and grandchildren, or travel to places you've never seen. Maybe you've decided house cleaning is not something you enjoy, so less space to clean is an attractive possibility. You could be concerned about the amount of maintenance your home needs and are ready to leave that responsibility behind.

Goals

A few years ago, a movie came out titled *The Bucket List*. For those who have not seen it, the story is about two men, each given a short time to live, who proceed to enjoy everything they had missed in life. The Bucket List was a list of these goals.

Various experts have offered their formula for goal-setting. However, it's simply about identifying what you wish to accomplish and working toward these goals. Part of the impetus to work toward goals is what's in it for you once each goal is achieved. Of course, there is a bit more to it.

It's important to write your goals on paper (the objective you're aiming for), sign and date the paper. There will be obstacles to achieving your goals, so recognize and work around them. What resources will you need? An action plan will help you identify them. Perhaps you haven't all the knowledge you need. Investigate this so you're educated enough to continue.

Remember that there's a pay-off or reward once you've reached each goal. Focus on that to keep you going. And work on only one goal at a time so you're not overwhelmed.

How does this apply to downsizing? Think about how keeping unused stuff can be a shrine to unmet goals. Do you need that reminder—all those "just in case" items, the unread books, the unworn clothes bought on a whim?

What do we really want from life? Here's a sample worksheet to help decide. Add lines as needed.

Goals Worksheet:

GOAL (what do I need to do?)	ACTION PLAN (how can I do it?)	STEPS (how can I get there?)	COMPLETION DATE (deadline)	REWARD ☺
e.g. lost 20 lbs.	Bring only healthy food into my home	Shop with a list	August 20 this year	I'll fit into that fabulous outfit I've been wanting.

Plan

"If you're not moving toward a goal,
you're running in place."
~ Anon

Remind yourself why you're downsizing. Keep the goals you've identified in mind throughout the process.

It's OK to have a temporary "keep" box if you're unsure of items. Just don't let it become your fall-back position for everything.

It's also normal to change your mind sometimes. Make sure, though, this doesn't morph into waffling rather than decision-making.

Moving to an apartment or condominium offers more options. You will be able to enjoy the benefits of a simpler life, have freedom from the concerns of maintaining a large property, and more mobility without worrying about leaving an empty house when you travel. And you won't have so many places to search for a missing item.

The benefits of a simpler life are clear. You could experience more peace, freedom and control in your life. You might even feel better and have a more optimistic outlook on life. You might feel liberated once much of your stuff is gone.

Another way to look at this, is that if you deal with your own weeding out, you will not be leaving a huge burden to your children or whomever else will have to deal with this after you're gone.

Amanda is an example. Already in her 70s, she was dealing with two estates simultaneously. The stress of this caused her to think about the work she would be leaving her children if she didn't deal with her own belongings while she was able. This was a wise thought on her part. It's difficult enough to lose someone you love without having the extra anxiety of deciding what to do with his or her belongings.

Or, if you can't decide what to do with them, and you must move, your children will be burdened with everything until you do decide. Conversely, you may be the adult child who warehouses your parents' goods.

With the celebration of her 80th birthday, her children asked Kate about clearing out some of her collections. They lived several hours away and were concerned about their mother tripping on scatter mats, forgetting food in the bottom of a large freezer and about having so much stuff in general. Kate was unwilling to let anything go from her large home, saying her children could take care of everything when she is gone.

Something for the single person to think about: Who will take care of all that you've carefully accumulated when you're unable to do it yourself?

Life isn't a game in which the one who dies with the most toys (or stuff) wins.

Where to start?

There are two places in a house worth thinking about first. The basement is the foundation of your home. If it's disorganized and messy, chances are your whole home is too. The attic is over your head. If it's disorganized and messy, your thoughts likely will be, as well.

First, decide what you really need. Be ruthless about your decisions. Check the top shelves—that's often where items are stored and forgotten. If your treadmill has become a place to hang clothing to dry, it can go. If you decide to work out in the future, either purchase another one if you have space, or join a gym where you can enjoy being with others, and maybe make new friends.

It's easiest to begin downsizing areas of your home you don't use much, like the hidden storage spaces—under the bed, attic, or spare bedroom, even your clothes closet, or linen cupboard. Start where the emotional value is least in order to get a running start on the project. You'll be surprised how much is stashed away that you can't see. Don't forget your junk drawer and bathroom cabinets, as well as those top shelves.

Are you storing things that belong to others? Many parents keep items their children have left behind when they moved to university or their own apartment. Sometimes we kindly agree to temporarily store things for other family members or friends and that extends to years. A wise person once said that parents are never empty-nesters as long as they're storing their children's belongings.

Set a deadline for everything to be removed and reclaim your space. Don't hesitate or you won't let anything go. Now that you're downsizing, this is good motivation for others to remove their possessions.

What to do?

Pick a place—the room least used. Work your way around the room, removing the big items first to make space for sorting the rest. By doing this, you will see accomplishment faster and provide momentum to continue.

Why these places specifically? Because it's easier to give the boot to items with less sentimental attachment, and you'll create space to work your way through the contents of other rooms.

Have you kept dozens of empty margarine containers or plastic grocery bags? Get rid of them immediately. You *do* know they multiply behind closed cabinet doors! Or if you have a collection of magazines you've been meaning to read and haven't, the recycling bin will be pleased to take them away. If this is too difficult, distribute the magazines around town to waiting rooms or donate them to the public library.

Letting go of belongings can be more difficult than you think. I recently began a downsizing exercise myself and was surprised how difficult it was. The hardest part was letting go of books. My mind was in gear but my emotions weren't. Giving books away is hard for me. I hadn't reached the stage where "books belonged to a person I had outgrown . . . eventually they turned into wallpaper."[3]

This is an interesting point about books, now that I think of it. A few years ago, I passed on my childhood collection of story books titled *My Bookhouse*. They went to a relative who had little children at the time, and she was thrilled to have the books because they were so different from those on the market today. Containing stories with old-fashioned values, they suited her.

At that time, many boxes of books left my home. That purge was less difficult than it is today. Those books didn't nourish my heart and soul. They were just bound paper and their departure only meant I had more space.

I did, however, keep books that were meaningful to me—the comfortable old friends I read over and over again, the ones that inspire me.

Do books, videos, CDs, DVDs etc. represent who you are now? Do they hold happy memories of a person, place or time? Or are they throwbacks to a previous life that's long gone? Is there room to keep all of them?

Clothes

"Getting rid of old clothes is like shedding old skin."
~ Carol Hathaway (Psychologist)

Some seem to have a more emotional attachment to clothes than others. Many women I know still have their wedding dress, and they've been married for decades! Even after divorce, some women keep their wedding dress.

Another category of clothing women tend to keep is bridesmaid dresses with the matching satin shoes. If you've been a bridesmaid repeatedly, these dresses can take a lot of space you could use for clothing you actually wear now.

Is something you wore for . . . (fill in the blank . . .) occasion still in your closet? Time to let it go if you're not wearing it once in a while. A closet that's escaped being organized for many years might look like a child's dress-up trunk.

I'm reminded of two cases that fit this situation. When she was forced to move due to poor health, Martha still had every coat she ever owned. And Jess, now in her 50s, had every pair of shoes she wore in adulthood, still in their boxes some 25 years later! Of course most of them, both coats and shoes, didn't fit their owners and were long out of style. But they had become like family. Letting any of them go was emotionally difficult.

Make peace with your past. Ask yourself why you're keeping things. Recognize that clothes can be a substitute for something missing from your life. Try to resolve this and let them go.

Think how good it will feel to know everything in your closet fits you and you look great wearing it. Having a few good quality items will see you through many years. Consider this an investment in your future.

I'll fit into them someday

Then there are the clothes that don't fit. You tell yourself you will lose weight and then you'll already have a wardrobe. Or you keep the larger size in case you gain weight. Neither of these is a good reason to keep clothes.

My client, Melissa, a professional woman, had five descending sizes of clothes because she "was going to fit into them when she lost weight." That was almost six years ago, and they're still hanging in her closet, unworn.

In fact, I did this myself a number of years ago. When I could finally fit into all those wonderful fashions again, I realized I didn't like them after all. I'd been dragging them around with me for years, through at least four moves! What a waste of space and effort!

Treat yourself to new clothes when your current ones are too big—AND get the bigger ones out of your home so you're not temped to grow back into them. Downsizing is the time to do it. Your new closets will likely be smaller than the ones you have now, so purge those clothing memories (or are they nightmares?) and start fresh.

Focus on the present—wearing clothes you have now and letting go of wardrobes past. Think of how liberated and light you'll feel.

Too much

The other side of this is worth recognizing, as well. Years ago when I worked in the fashion industry, I observed how we are coerced into filling our closets with the latest of everything. Some people I knew then completely changed their wardrobe every season because what they wore the previous season was out of style. Horrors!

Remember Pareto's Principle? Maybe you know it as the 80/20 Rule. We wear 20 per cent of our clothes 80 per cent of the time. Are those 80 per cent worth the amount of closet space they occupy? Remember Imelda Marcos and her thousands of pairs of shoes? Let's not fall into that trap.

"Simplicity is the ultimate sophistication."
~ Leonardo DaVinci (1452-1519, Artist)

New lifestyle

Another consideration regarding clothes is that once we retire from the workplace, our wardrobe requirements change, as well. We no longer need business attire, and are probably adding more casual clothing. Why fill our closet with things we never wear? Keeping a few outfits makes sense. But keeping all of them is living in the past and occupying prime real estate we cannot afford.

Once you've purged your closets and there's actually room in them to be able to move the hangers along the bar easily, resist the urge to refill them. Think of how much less ironing you'll have to do when your clothes aren't squeezed together!

Craft, sewing, knitting supplies

This is another set of collections many women need to deal with. In a larger home, there's space to spread out and work on these, if we, in fact, still do. From experience, I can tell you these are addictive. We see fabric that we love, or on sale, or needed for a particular reason or event, and we buy it. Then circumstances change. We don't make the garment or quilt, and the fabric sits, joining the other pieces saved for the right time. Suddenly we have a room full of fabric, trims, buttons and such.

Likewise, craft and knitting supplies multiply just as sewing supplies do. Unfinished projects will take up space that we will need for living in our new, smaller home. Time to let at least some of them go to a happier home. Think about donating such supplies to schools, summer camps, Girl Guides etc.

Linens

Beds come and go, but somehow bed linens don't accompany them. Do you have sheets and blankets for beds you no longer own? Time to pass them on. This should be easy because there's no real reason to keep them. For the beds you do have, three sets of bed linens are plenty. That goes for blankets and towels, as well. The local animal shelter will be pleased to take any extras off your hands.

Encyclopedia Sets

These could have gone to the recycling bin years ago. The information in them is long outdated, with the Internet as the main research source today. Yes, they may look educated sitting on a shelf, but remember, you're downsizing. That means less space in your future to store such items. Just pull the covers off—recycling usually doesn't want these.

Emotional Value

Why does an item hold emotional value? Maybe because it represents an especially meaningful family event (the topper for your wedding cake) or information (books), or childhood (Bunnykins dishes, your silver baby cup). When you're considering what to take with you, share the story of the special items with someone who will appreciate your memories. One caution here though: Don't assume other people will share your deep feelings about your treasures. Memories can hold more importance in your heart and mind than the item itself may indicate.

For the men reading this, I've seen plenty of ragged, dirty high school football and hockey jackets in clients' homes that seemingly cannot be parted with. The only reason I can think of for this is they hold emotional value their owners are not ready to deal with.

For Florence, a move into a smaller apartment necessitated letting go of many treasures. Sentimental things, especially anything that reminded her of when her children were small, were most difficult to part with. She did finally let some go, but not all. As long as there was space for the items she did keep, she felt she could do so without cramming those treasures into places they didn't fit. Another person may have made a different decision.

Are we there yet?

If you look back, you'll probably note that this is a lifetime of accumulation so it can't be purged overnight.

> *"A journey of a thousand miles begins with a single step."*
> ~ Confucius (551 BC-479 BC, Philosopher)

Downsizing is a process most of us repeat several times in our lives. It's streamlining our homes in a variety of ways as we plan for the future while we enjoy the present. We learn to let go of the past.

Steps

Assess your home's contents

Decide what will fit into your new home. If it's half the size of your current home, you need to eliminate half of what you have. Likewise, if your new place is one quarter the size of your home now, you need to let three quarters go. Yes, this may be drastic and difficult, but it's reality. Try to think of how much easier it will be to maintain fewer belongings. Focus on the upside—positive shrinking.

Create an action plan

Write the steps you need to take for this project and put this paper into a 3-ring binder, so it's easier to carry along with you (or an electronic note pad if you have one). Add dividers and paper. Using the dividers, section the binder into timeline, ideas, quotes (for moving, new furniture, transferring your telephone etc.), future needs, and anything else pertaining to your project. Write everything down so you know at which stage you are at any time.

Consider that if you move unneeded items that cannot be organized in your new place, you will pay more to the movers, both to get these items to your new place and then to remove them. They charge by the amount of time it takes to load and unload the van, as well as for weight on a long-distance relocation. So, to save money, offload anything you don't need now.

Gillian's husband had been working across the country for two years when it became time for her to pack up the household, children and cats to join him. It was especially difficult because she and her husband built their house. She remembers standing in the hole that became the basement and working with him during construction, bringing babies to that home, and the sacred pet cemetery in the back garden.

Downsizing for Gillian meant letting go of almost everything in order to control the moving costs. She found it difficult to do this as she felt she had just reached the point in life where she had finally furnished her home in an adult fashion. Starting over didn't appeal to her, even though she tried to see the light at the end of the tunnel.

Stressed didn't begin to describe her feelings. However, Gillian found the more she purged, the easier it became.

The hardest part can be deciding what to keep. Start with those items you really love. Let go of high-maintenance belongings, such as fine china, crystal etc. unless you use them often. My rule of thumb is that if it doesn't go into the dishwasher, I don't want it. And I'm hearing this more often from friends and acquaintances.

Keep items that are meaningful, necessary and irreplaceable. Keep the comfortable furniture. Let go of extra lamps and everyday dishes. Use the good ones in future.

Some years ago, I visited a relative who lived far away from any city. I was surprised to see she used her Royal Doulton china all the time and thought how practical this was, not to mention feeling that every meal was special and to be enjoyed to the fullest.

Instead of packing every piece of a collection, select your favorite pieces and let the rest go. Of your collection of 100 cookbooks, I suspect there are probably 10 or 15 you use regularly? Or six dozen wine glasses? One dozen would probably be enough to keep.

Lorna collected antique glassware for decades. Recently she decided she needed to begin downsizing her collection in preparation for a future move to smaller quarters. Keeping a few small pieces and one larger piece, she gave away the balance. Her theory is that, "If I move to a place where these pieces will fit, I'll keep all of them. If not, I'll keep what fits and get rid of the rest." She acknowledges that as long as she can enjoy looking at a few pieces, or even only one piece, she will be happy.

You might take photos of the whole collection before passing on most of it. Then you could look at the pictures any time to enjoy how the collection looked together.

This is a good time to have valuable items evaluated for insurance purposes, and to have a rider added to your home policy to cover them should tragedy occur. If you then decide to sell them, you will know their real value and what price to expect.

Downsizing Worksheet:

KEEP	DONATE	GIVE TO FAMILY	TOSS
e.g. my favorite china	Extra linens, bedding, etc.	The china I don't like, if they want it.	Chipped dishes.

Download full-sized worksheets at
www.goforwarddownsize.com/specialgift.

List what you must take with you, what you might take with you

Keep the "Must" and "Might" items. Get rid right away of what you definitely don't need. You have no room for extras. Sacrifices and compromise are part of the decision-making process, as hard as this may be.

- Clear one room to work in and set up areas for Keep (MUST), Keep (MIGHT), Give Away, Sell and Garbage. (You will be surprised to find you do have garbage.)
- Give items to family and friends first to create working space to continue. Start with the larger pieces both so you feel a sense of accomplishment, and to create more work space.
- Keep garbage bags handy and remove the full ones as you go.
- Allow plenty of time for sorting so you can make thoughtful decisions and feel good about them.
- Color code bags so you don't throw away anything valuable: Black for garbage, clear for donations, blue for recycling. If you prefer to use only one type of bag, choose the clear ones. Remember not to overload them.

Eliminate

Give away as much as you can. Shed everything that is no longer useful to you.

Storage

What storage exists in your new place? What will fit into it? Of course you'll be taking off-season clothes, kitchen supplies, and maybe some tools etc. with you, and all this will need to be stored somewhere. Ensure there's enough room in your new place for the items you plan to take with you.

Use up food before you move, and stop buying anything but perishables as soon as you've decided on a move date. Decide who you will give the remainder to if you do have food left before a long move.

If you happen to have bulk quantities of paper or other goods that cannot be used before the big day, consider giving them away because your storage will likely be too small to keep all of it. Consider giving them to a food bank. They can always use donations.

Focus on your goal

Visualize the finished space with your furniture in it, or with some new furniture (maybe what you have now is too large or needs repair, or you decide it's time for a change). Envision every item in its new place and think about whether you'll still feel good about it in a few years. If the answer is negative, let it go now. Imagine how much easier it will be to live in a place where you can enjoy life rather than spending your time cleaning and repairing. We will discuss ways to do this later.

By creating physical space around you, you're opening the door for new experiences to come in.

Pace yourself

Don't spend more than four hours each day working on this if you have a choice. It's exhausting and overwhelming. The exhaustion is both physical and emotional. With the rest of the day, arrange for pickup of things going to charity, reward yourself for a job well done and get plenty of rest. And remember to eat regular, healthy meals to keep your strength up.

If you're inclined to lose track of time, set a timer to break up the hours you plan to work into smaller chunks.

Memory Lane

Sorting treasures can be an enjoyable trip down memory lane. But it also can be emotional and tiring. Treasures hold years of memories, deeper than the item might indicate. Do you still feel the attachment? Take time to recall memories and shed tears as you need to. This can be both healing and cathartic. As mentioned earlier, work with someone who understands so you can share stories as you go. Your nostalgic stories can be a gift to the person who helps you.

> *"That which you cannot give away, you do not possess.*
> *It possesses you."*
> ~ Ivern Ball (Poet, Author)

Break the Spell

Focus on the future, break the spell—don't let stuff you've collected in the past hold you there. Work on comparing today's lifestyle with what you expect tomorrow's lifestyle to be. Celebrate this new stage in life. Stop watching life through your rear-view mirror. Not to say holding memories is bad. In fact, they make life richer. However, living only in the past indicates little personal growth.

Once you've let go, you'll feel more relaxed with fewer responsibilities and fewer things to keep track of. Life will be richer when you're not focusing on possessions. If you're comfortable with yourself, you might not need as much as you thought you did. Your attitude makes all the difference in the ease and success of your project! Take time to nourish your soul.

Give stuff away to allow space for new, positive life changes.

New Beginnings

Ask yourself how little you can live with so you'll be comfortable in your home. You don't have to move physically to begin anew. You may simply want to create more space in your current residence. A journey to the future, unencumbered by unnecessary stuff can be spiritually liberating. The awareness that our surroundings nourish us affirms that we are on the right track.

> *"You have succeeded in life when all you really want*
> *is only what you really need."*
> ~ Vernon Howard (1818-1992 Teacher, Author, Philosopher)

Who gets what?

There's not much in life that can tear a family apart faster than a perceived injustice when it comes to inheritances. While you can, discuss the future with your family and friends so there are no misunderstandings or complaints of favoritism. It might be a good idea to invite everyone to your home at the same time so they all hear the same information.

Fortunately, this doesn't happen all the time. Margot tells of how she and her sisters were responsible for dealing with their parents' home, its contents and inhabitants. As they got along well, they were able to work together. And after two months' preparation, the house sold in only two weeks.

The sisters took another two weeks to remove the remainder of the contents, taking what furniture and other items they wanted, while an auction house took most of the rest. Once other items were sold, they received a check for 60 per cent of what the auction house received. Items the auctioneer did not take were donated.

They also found homes for two cats and two dogs.

Emphasize to family and friends that you aren't planning on leaving this world any time soon, or guaranteeing their choices, but that you need a guideline for downsizing. Not discussing this won't make the issue go away. With the evaluation in hand, you can ensure everyone receives items worth approximately the same value.

Start by having an evaluator assess every item. Then ask your family and friends what they would like from your estate. You may be surprised to learn you've been saving items you thought they would treasure and they don't really care about after all. Janet and David accepted donations from their parents that they didn't want, and felt responsible to dispose of the items. Their home had become impossibly cluttered and they began to feel guilty about not wanting everything they had received. That's not the best way to divest yourself of your belongings.

Remember, the main purpose is to simplify your life and make space in it for new experiences such as travel, enjoying an activity you've been postponing, or even making new friends.

"A little simplification would be the first step toward rational living, I think."
~ Eleanor Roosevelt (1884-1962 in *My Days*)

Just to remind you—be sure to check with family before giving anything away. Anna was moving from a three-bedroom home to a two-bedroom apartment. Knowing she had to eliminate a fair quantity of items from her home, she sent everything off to charity without checking with family members first. Many were hurt they didn't have the chance to claim special dishes and other items from their mother's and grandmother's home.

Passing on your treasures can be a time to:

- Celebrate your life
- Share memories and stories
- Continue traditions and family history

If you leave these decisions for others to deal with, what happens may not accurately reflect your wishes. Sometimes, more than one person believes they have been promised the same item.

Once you have in writing what items each member of your family would like to have from your estate, give them those things you're not using. For the remainder:

- Make a list and attach to your Will (you will want to update your Will once you've given away some items and your home is sold, if you're selling it).
- Be specific and use a name and relationship: "I want my second son, Jason William, to have my coin collection. My porcelain doll collection goes to my friend, Jane

Jones." Describe the item if there's any doubt. Attach a photo of the item. Date and sign the paper.[4]

- Pass on family stories that go with the items. Consider writing the stories and/or recording them on CD or DVD. You may think your children know that the pocket watch had been passed on to each generation of men named William in the family since 1792, but maybe they don't. Besides, having your words for posterity is a gift in itself.

Ways to Divest

- Options include family, friends, contents sale, charity, auction.
- Once your family and friends have chosen the items they want to remember you by, you could hold an open house to sell the remainder. You know the value because you already have the evaluator's report.
- If more than one person wants an item, they could draw for it.
- Valuable items can be given to a charity that may auction them and give you a tax receipt for price paid by the highest bidder.
- Or hire an estate liquidator to auction them. The fee charged is usually a percentage of the final sales total.

Food for thought:

Do you want to be remembered for your possessions or for yourself? Give those following you the gift of dealing with your belongings yourself rather than leaving that difficult task to them.

More food for thought:

- As the population ages, there will be an oversupply of antiques, causing the price to drop. This has already started to happen. Sell them now if you can.
- Keeping the memory and letting the object go is a process of growth.
  There's no point in keeping these things in order to sell them for a higher price in a few years. Take a photo of heirlooms and sentimental pieces, write down your memories about them and give them away. You can relive the memories with what you have kept, and this will take less space than the item itself. Also, the recipient will appreciate knowing its history.
- Hidden boxes and bags hold a multitude of unfiled old photos, letters and diaries.

Photos

As you find photos in your downsizing project, toss them into a laundry basket or large box to sort later. They will be safe there for the time being and not slow down your progress.

When you do reach the time when you can deal with them, purge those you wouldn't put in an album. You know the ones—photos of someone's feet when the camera went off unexpectedly, and out-of-focus photos.

Write on the back the names of those in the photo, the place it was taken and the date. If you have children or siblings, make a photo box for each person and sort the pictures to give to each of them at a later date. This will get them out of your space and give them a wonderful memory. It might generate conversation too, and encourage you to tell them your memories of those occasions.

If you have a family historian, give the remainder to that person because they can be useful for family history and genealogical purposes. You may have some very old photos that no one can identify. Consider having them digitized along with the ones you are keeping. At some point in the future, someone may be able to identify the old ones that are precious to your family genealogy.

If you are not computerized, ask your children or grandchildren to scan them for you, identifying the file with as much information about the content as you know. Alternatively, take them to a reputable photo finisher for scanning. They can then be burned onto a CD, and even copies made for those who want them. If the hard photos are stuck in boxes where no one can enjoy seeing them, they're forgotten and will deteriorate over time.

Having a digitized file on your computer is good. However, burning a CD or memory stick with the files, and keeping it in your safety deposit box is equally important. Should your computer suffer a disaster, the photos will still be safe.

If you prefer to have photo albums or scrapbooks, by all means create them. Just be sure you have a backup safely protected.

Letters and diaries

Letters and diaries that may contain embarrassing information about you or others can be shredded. However, if any of these might be of interest to your children or grandchildren, either give them to them now or package them up for your children to have later.

You might want to scan the letters and diaries too, for safekeeping. And don't forget documents that give details about an ancestor's life. They are a gold mine of information to the family genealogist in their original form. Scan them too, but keep the originals in a safe place, preferably your safety deposit box with your other important documents. Have a copy available to show if anyone is interested.

Display the good stuff

There are many choices when it comes to displaying treasures so you can enjoy them regularly. Photos can be arranged as a collage in a large frame. A shadow box can display military medals, a baseball glove or baby's christening clothes. There are beautiful table-top display cases available now in which items such as rings, pocket watches, reading glasses and the like can be placed. Even a special T-shirt can be made into a cushion for the owner to remember the occasion when it was new.

It's important that someone neutral (someone with no vested interest in the items) helps you or your elder go through the sorting of memories and the tangible goods associated with them. Telling the stories helps underline their importance and may make it easier to let go of the items themselves.

How to eliminate non-essentials

Ask yourself:

- Do I love and use this item?
- Will I ever use it again?
- Have I tried on ALL my clothes lately?
- Do they fit?
- Do I feel good in them?
- Does each piece still fit my lifestyle?
- Would I save it if my house were burning down?
- Does someone in my family attach personal value to it?
- Could someone else benefit from having it more than I do?

Once you've gone through this checklist, anything that doesn't answer the questions positively can go. The last question, of course, answers the questions above it, and that answer is usually "yes."

Nadia used the checklist for her collection of Norman Rockwell decorative plates. At the time of her first move she'd been collecting them for 14 years. When time came for her fifth move, she still had those plates and decided it was time to give them away. She admitted, "I never really liked them anyway!"

> *"Have nothing in your houses that you do not know to be useful or believe to be beautiful."*
> ~ William Morris (1834-1896 Artist, Writer)

If you're working with family and/or friends at this point, here are some important things to consider:

- Remember the 80/20 Rule.
- Work methodically. Focus on one room or part of a room at a time so you're not distracted and will therefore accomplish more.
- Empty the room frequently to have space to work. Take care stuff doesn't sprout legs and walk back to where it was. The boxes containing the "Keep" items can now be packed well, contents listed, sealed and moved to a safe place.
- Donate books to your local library; send clothes to consignment or charity. Other items could go to schools, hospitals, churches, women's shelters or the museum.
- When this is complete, move to the next room. Continue packing as you go.

If working around a room is too daunting, begin with a shelf or drawer. As you feel more motivated, then move to a room, and focus on only one part at a time.

4. Downsizing Others

Others can be parents, friends or relatives. Helping friends downsize is different from helping your parents. Health is a major consideration for any downsizing. If the downsizer is in good health and can participate, the project is easier. Depending on their ability to be involved, you will need to proceed a bit differently. Can they make their own decisions? Do they understand why this is necessary and accept the reasons?

The activity of downsizing is much the same regardless of who is doing it. The same questions apply, whether an item is loved, useful, in good repair and fits the space available.

Things to remember:

- The stuff is theirs.
- Basic downsizing for others is same as for self.
- Allow plenty of time. Seniors have a longer walk down memory lane to relive memories. And they may move a little slower along the way.
- If they are moving, move familiar items with them, if possible.

Your elder needs to make his/her own decisions about where their belongings go (consider a short-term storage unit if necessary). Having familiar items in the new place is important so they feel it's really theirs. This applies to furniture (if possible), artwork (including pictures for the walls), memorabilia and so on.

The most important thing to remember is to be understanding of their situation and feelings. Everyone must work at his or her own pace; don't force your timeline on them. If necessary, you can always put the remainder into storage to be completed later.

Go back to the reason for downsizing. What is the situation at hand? Why are they moving? Has their health deteriorated? Do they need care that is best provided in a retirement home or care facility? Or do they simply need to be closer to conveniences?

It can still be a difficult transition, especially if the elder isn't ready to move into a smaller place or care facility. Sometimes the decision is made for them, if they have an accident or degenerative disease causing them to be unable to live alone. It's always best if they can make their own decisions and understand why. It also can be emotional for you while helping them.

Needs when downsizing another

If you are fully responsible for the other person's downsizing and moving, you will need knowledge in a few areas you would not normally need.

- What are their resources—financial, family, friends, neighbors, faith community and community organizations?
- Knowing their financial situation is important so you can help them understand what rent they can afford. Chances are the more elderly the person, the more difficult it will be for them to understand the cost of

apartments compared to what they may have paid 50 years ago.

- Legal considerations:
  This is a conversation you will need to have when you're responsible for someone. Encourage him or her to make an appointment with a lawyer to take care of the following:

  a) Up-to-date Will—Remind them to indicate in their Will whom they want to receive valuable items, according the lists made earlier. It's important to be specific as to whom each item will go. Ensure they use the person's name and relationship along with the item. If you can arrange for a photo of the item to be attached, this will make probate much easier.

  b) Power of Attorney for Personal Care and Power of Attorney for Property—If your friend or relative needs someone to make decisions for them when they're unable, it's important that the legal side of this is in place. Otherwise, a government agency will take over this process giving you no say about what happens.

Seniors

When moving seniors, know that it's a unique process. There will likely be as many reactions as there are people involved. However, the main goal is to eliminate as much stress and frustration as possible for them. They may be uncomfortable with change, for example.

Change

The French have a wonderful phrase for change—*"partir se mourir un peu"*—when we move, a little of us dies.

Change can be difficult especially if we're not the one who decided to make the change. It takes effort and activity to make it happen. We might be apprehensive about the unknown, what's outside our comfort zone.

In her famous book *On Death and Dying*, Elizabeth Kubler-Ross outlined the various stages one can go through when grieving. These can easily be applied to any change situation.

When moving is the change, we may go through:

- Denial (This can't really be happening—I'll ignore it and it will go away)
- Anger (Who do they think they are, telling me I have to move?)
- Acceptance (realization that it may not be such a bad idea after all)

To manage change, we need to be able to let go of what we can't control. Maybe we don't even know what we're hanging onto. The important thing is to communicate our feelings and thoughts to those close to us. By allowing ourselves to be open to new possibilities, the situation can improve. It's actually an opportunity for growth, a new beginning.

> *"We all have big changes in our lives*
> *that are more or less a second chance."*
> ~ Harrison Ford (Actor, Producer)

If we can focus on what we're gaining instead of what we're losing; if we can look on this as an adventure, it may become easier.

Attitude

We're responsible for our own attitude about everything. To make positive changes, we need to trust, love and respect ourselves—an attitude adjustment. Conversely, by holding onto the thoughts of loss, all we're doing is creating pain for ourselves, and who needs more of that?

II NEW HOME

1. Your New Home

Needs

- Has your lifestyle changed?
- Are there rooms in your current home you seldom or never use?
- How many rooms do you really need?
- Are you concerned about the stairs? Maybe a bungalow or apartment is the answer. Will you need an elevator? (If possible, choose a building with more than one elevator so when one is down for major maintenance, you will still have access to the building's upper floors without climbing stairs.) What about security?

Location

Before deciding on your new place, is it

- Safe?
- Close to family and friends?
- Close to shopping, church, other activities you enjoy?
- Close to public transit?
- Equipped with the services you need? (mailbox, parking, laundry facilities . . .)

Consider:

- Bringing a friend or relative with you to help decide. They may notice a detail or problem you don't.
- Is there a sense of community in the neighborhood or building?
- Is it clean and well-maintained?

- Choose your apartment or condo before downsizing so you'll know how much to keep that will fit into it, unless you plan to start with everything new.

Furniture Arrangement

- Rooms will likely be smaller than those you have now, so it's a good idea to pre-arrange your furniture. You will want to measure each piece of furniture you wish to take with you, as well as the rooms into which they will be going. Note where the electrical outlets, telephone jacks, doors and windows are located.
- There are three options for working out what will fit where.

  o One:
    - Find a software program to help you arrange the furniture.
    - Place the furniture icons on the software room grid, taking care not to put them in front of doors or blocking electrical outlets.
    - Move the "pieces" around until you find a pleasing arrangement.
    - Print the final arrangement and give it to your movers so on delivery they can place the large pieces where you want them.

  o Two:
    - Draw up a floor plan to scale on graph paper, with one square on the paper as being equal to one foot of the space, using the dimensions you have determined (above). If this seems too small, use two squares per foot.

- Cut colored paper into shapes of your furniture, using the same scale as for the rooms.
- Move these around on the graph paper room outline to create a pleasing floor plan.
- Once this is done, make a copy for the movers.

o Three:
  - Mark out your new room space with tape on the floor of your current home for an accurate view of the finished room. Move your furniture into this space to see what will fit and how it will look.
  - Sketch this out for the movers.

Repurpose furniture: A dresser need not be only a bedroom piece. It could be used for storage in another room or as a sofa table with the drawers facing outwards. Two drawers, placed bottom to bottom on edge facing outward, can be a coffee table with magazines or books standing in them.

Freshen up special pieces by painting or having them refinished.

Leave about three feet between furniture pieces to be able to walk comfortably between them.

Sell or give away unnecessary pieces. If they have great value, consider having an expert appraisal. In order to be neutral, it's better if this person does not have a vested interest in the sale. Check e-Bay for similar items for an idea of what you might expect.

- o A yard sale is probably the most work of all the ways you may choose. See the section on this later.
- o Kijiji: Check the site for your own city to avoid shipping charges and buyers can take your items right away. Accept only cash for any sales.
- o e-Bay: This can be more work as shipping can be required. Check the website for details.
- o Craigslist: As above—shipping can be required. Check the website for details.
- o Consignment: If there is a place in your city that accepts items on consignment (clothing, household goods) verify what their rules are about quality and condition of your belongings before taking anything in. Some will accept only designer clothes that have not been altered and have just been cleaned; others aren't as specific. You can expect to receive 30 to 45 per cent of the selling price.
- o Estate Auction: Check your telephone book for an auctioneer in your area. Remember that the value you put on your goods will probably be more than an auctioneer will.
- o Donate to Goodwill, the Salvation Army, diabetes association or any other local charity. Some will pick up from you. Check with them directly.
- o Freecycle: Post your items there for someone to come and take away. No money changes hands. In your browser, type in your city's name to find the closest Freecycle.

- Replace large furniture with double-duty pieces that have built-in storage or space-savers e.g. sofa bed, Murphy bed, captain's or platform bed, nesting tables, footstools with removable lids, drawers under beds etc.

Remember the scale of your new place when buying. You might take along your floor plan to be sure the new pieces will fit with what you already have there.

- Consider having built-ins installed in your new place. They take less space than regular furniture and can house a multitude of your precious belongings.

- Add storage with window seats and shelving. You may add an extra one or two shelves to the top of your closet if there's enough space. Hang clothes on double rods. Create a second rod below the top one by drilling holes in a piece of plastic pipe a bit smaller diameter than a hanger hook, and feed chain or rope through the holes, then attach to the top rod. Raise the bed using risers found in organizing stores or home health care supplies stores to allow space to store bins under your bed.

- Make your new place gorgeous. This is your opportunity to change your color scheme, your style, and experiment with anything you've never done before. This is one secret to positive downsizing.

Supply the movers with your floor plan so they will place large furniture where you want it.

Yard/garage sale

While holding a yard/garage sale can be fun way to meet the neighbors and other shoppers, this is probably the most difficult way to dispose of items you no longer need. It can be more work than the profit is worth. Think carefully before undertaking this challenge.

If you do decide to go ahead with the sale, ensure items are clean, in good repair and well displayed on tables. You may consider throwing a plain table cloth or sheet over the table to display your items more attractively. Price every item with small stickers before sale day so there will be no unnecessary questions regarding price. Know that prospective buyers will nearly always offer much less than the sticker price. But that's a starting point.

Be sure to advertise well in order to attract the most traffic possible for your goods to sell better.

Decide ahead of time not to bring anything left over back into your home. Instead, pack it up and take it to a local charity store.

Plan that once you've taken down the tables and leftovers are gone, and everything is complete, to celebrate with a hot shower and maybe takeout dinner.

2. Another's New Home

Helping your friend or relative shop for a new home can be quite enjoyable. Are you looking at a smaller home, for example a two-bedroom house when the other person lives in a six-bedroom home? Maybe he or she has decided that living in a condo or apartment is a better choice at this time of life.

While some friends and relatives are still healthy and able to participate fully in this activity, others may not be. We refer to seniors and elders as those who need more help. However this is not necessarily an age-related situation.

Choosing a new home for a senior can be different from doing that for someone younger. With the prevalence of the youth culture, Botox and opportunities for seniors to be involved longer than they could a few decades ago, seniors are often healthier and more fit today. Despite all this, there are still some considerations to be aware of.

New Home for a senior

If a senior finds his or her home is too large, other living solutions are possible:

- Share living accommodations with a younger person.
- Move into a "granny" suite in someone else's home.
- Move into a retirement community.

Consider this decision for the long term and whether the elder will be able to maintain the new place five, 10 years or more from now. How would he/she react to having to move again, if necessary? Does the place you're considering offer the option of your elder remaining there when more care is needed? Has everyone concerned given this move sufficient thought?

Trade-offs may be necessary. It's possible that not all the desired amenities will be available. In addition, your elder may subconsciously or consciously feel he or she is downsizing independence as well as worldly goods. Be sensitive to this.

Try to plan ahead when possible so the senior has a voice in the decision. When moving to another independent living place, it might be easier to control the timeline. However, if they're going to a care facility, you may have only two days to move them in, so you'll have work to do at their home afterward.

At the same time, understand the other's fears and concerns. They will want to maintain control of their living arrangements. Perhaps they have even been thinking about moving to a smaller place already, and are closer to making such a decision than you believe.

Care Needs

This can be broken down to two basic categories: Those needing minimal care and those needing full care. Will he or she be able to participate in the decision-making process?

Minimal Care/Independent Living

It can be emotionally difficult when an elder moves to a smaller home. He or she may view this as an obvious sign of growing older and being less able, and begin to feel some depression. The more familiar belongings that can be moved with them, the easier it might be to adjust to new surroundings.

Get in touch with your own emotions about this early on. You may be surprised at their intensity. Run through the possibilities surrounding the situation so when the reality happens, you will be more ready to deal with your feelings.

If the conversations feel uncomfortable, it's important to start talking early. This way, the situation is less threatening for everyone when it's hypothetical or theoretical.

A situation that comes to mind is Mary who lived in a three-bedroom house. She downsized to a two-bedroom apartment, and then needing care that could not be provided there, moved to a care-giving center. This was traumatic to her family, who agonized over Mary's health, as well as her loss of independence and space. Adjustment took a long time for all of them.

Full Care

It is important to do your homework early to ensure a good match between your elder and the facility. Be realistic about what's happening, and involve all family members in the decision making to avoid misunderstandings. Call a family meeting early in the process so you can come to a consensus. This may take more time than you expect, but it is crucial for everyone to agree on some level that a full-care facility is the right decision. Remember, this is for the health and safety of your elder, not yourself.

Check out different care facilities; compare amenities, costs, floor plans, bathrooms, dining rooms, available activities, transportation to shopping, banking etc. Talk with current residents about their feelings about the place. Eat in the dining room if you can in order to taste for yourself what the meals will be like. Compare and decide which place would be most suitable.

There may be a long wait list for a place in the facility of your preference. Take this into consideration and plan ahead. Find out what is required to add the name of your loved one to the list (How long is the wait list? Is a deposit necessary? Do you need references?).

Suzanna's father-in-law, Stan, wasn't sure he wanted to move into a seniors' residence. However, he finally allowed her to help. Suzanna hired Professional Organizers to pack and move his favorite things to the residence while she and her husband entertained Stan for the day. Everything not moved was kept in the family home so he could ask for anything else to come along if he chose. After a few weeks, Stan was content and the remaining contents of his home were sold or given away.

The important thing for Stan was that he was able to decide, when he was ready, what he wanted with him. Likewise, he was also able to decide when to let the remainder go.

Loss of control of one's life and loss of independence can precipitate depression. An elder in a situation not of their own choosing can easily fall into this. Adjustments from a previous life can be difficult, especially if he or she is dependent on others for daily living such as taking medication or when meals are served.

On the other hand, your senior may feel safer and more secure when someone else takes responsibility for daily living, whether this is in a care facility or someone coming into their home.

"As parents age, you must remember that many of their peers are dead. Their world becomes narrower and narrower and the attention of their children becomes, in the parent's mind, essential."[1] When asked about her friends, Rose, a mid-80s woman, responded with surprise, "Oh, I guess they're all dead." This is another reason for you to stay in close touch with a parent or elder for whom you're responsible. Loneliness is just as real for them as it is for someone younger.

III MOVING

We know moving is physically and emotionally tiring. It's hard work and stressful, even if it proceeds like clockwork. Allow plenty of time so you don't exhaust yourself. Take breaks during this process and focus on all the positives ahead. And, be gentle with yourself. It will get better.

Take care when placing items in your new home where anyone could trip over them. It is not uncommon for accidents to happen during or shortly after a move as we're getting used to our new place.

1. Moving Self

If you must pack before downsizing, pack and move only the essentials. Go back later to decide what will happen with the remainder, or move these items to a temporary storage unit if you can't return to complete the sorting.

If you're moving into an apartment building or condominium, be sure to reserve use of the elevator for several hours so there's no delay in taking boxes and furniture to their destination. Also remember to check about space for the moving van to park while unloading.

Moving with children

Even a smooth move can be more challenging than we'd like. Imagine how much more difficult it will be for children who may not fully understand what's happening. If they could spend moving day with friends or other family, it will be easier on both you and them. You could bring them home in time for a celebratory dinner after everything is in, the beds are made and the movers have gone.

Moving with seniors

In this case, it's not the elder who is moving to his/her own place, but in with family. Like moving with children, it may be better for your elder to spend the day with friends or other family so they don't have to deal with more stress than necessary. Once their room is set up, coming home to it will feel, well, like home.

Moving with pets

Helena, one of my clients, had two cats and a dog. She asked me to take care of the packing, unpacking and settling in for her. The animals were interesting, as well as entertaining. The cats liked to help pack, and even climbed into the boxes to ensure they were good enough for their person's belongings. They liked to play with the packing paper, as well.

The dog evoked gales of laughter from Helena and me the evening she carefully removed every one of her toys from the box I'd placed them in earlier in the day. I don't know how the dog knew where the toys had been in the room, but she returned each one to that location.

All this is to say that moving is stressful for Fido and Fluffy as well. Be sure to give them extra attention so they feel secure in their new home.

If at all possible, have your furry friends spend moving day at a kennel or with a trusted friend. They will be less anxious and more inquisitive when they join you in your new home.

2. Moving Another

When helping a friend or healthy relative to move, they will probably be as involved in the process as you are. Certainly, lending a hand is easier than taking full responsibility for someone who is unable to be involved in the hands-on parts of a move.

In this first case, all you will need to do is pitch in and provide moral support. Or, if circumstances are such that the person moving is not available, then more responsibility would fall to you. Everything we have discussed so far will apply.

In either case, there are a few things to remember:

- Always check with them for any decisions needing to be made.
- If they can be present and want to be there, find a way for them to be there.
- Have the furniture arrangement plan, tote with moving hardware in it, important telephone numbers, bottles of water, etc. with you to simplify the situation.

These days, many children live far from their parents, resulting in the parents needing someone trustworthy to help them through many of life's challenges, including moving.

Moving seniors who need extra care

Moving elders can be an especially delicate process. Your goal is to eliminate stress and frustration for everyone involved. One way to do this is to minimize the choices. Two choices are better than three.

It can be difficult to see someone we love placed in a care facility. Emotions can run high, including good old guilt. You may take it on yourself or there might be an attempt to impose it on you. Recognize what's happening so it doesn't consume you.

Involve your loved one in the process as much as possible. They might be resisting because they remember their parents or grandparents moving against their will. Old vocabulary often referred to this as "putting them away"—certainly a cause for anxiety.

Once moved, you may want to pay extra attention to your senior until he or she settles in and makes new friends. At some point, you may realize you've switched roles with your parent, and this can evoke strong emotions for you both. If you live far away, this exacerbates the situation.

If you can spend a bit more time with your senior for a while after the move, he or she will appreciate it. You may arrange a family dinner after moving in your senior so she or he will not feel abandoned once you leave for the night.

Often, once older folks are in a facility where they can associate with others and have regular nourishing meals, their physical health and mental outlook will improve. This will help all of you see the move more positively.

Usually some personal belongings can be moved into a care facility, but very few due to lack of space. Choose furniture carefully both for function and size.

If your elder is going to a place where laundry is included, take only clothing that is easy-care. Without someone to help, Elsie took wool slacks with her to the nursing home where she soon needed full care. After the slacks went through the wash, they were unwearable. Industrial machines eat clothes.

3. Packing

"Begin at the beginning," the King said gravely,
"and go till you come to the end; then stop."
~ Lewis Carroll (1832-1898, Alice's Adventures in Wonderland)

Being organized for your move considerably reduces stress. There are steps that, once taken, facilitate this.

- Allow at least eight weeks if possible to prepare for moving. There's less stress when you can proceed slowly and methodically so nothing is forgotten.
- Decide on a date.
- Create a Packing/Moving Log so you have everything you need in one place. You could add to the binder you used earlier for creating your action plan.
- Personalize the Appendix on page 107 to suit your needs. (Download additional pages from www.goforwarddownsize.com/specialgift) Print, punch holes in the pages and add to your Packing/Moving Log. To prevent possible theft, don't list the contents on the outside of the box. Punch holes in large envelopes and add them to your binder to hold any receipts you collect that pertain to your move.
- Continue listing in the appropriate section of your Log what you would like to purchase for your new home, where to get it, the cost, if it's a special order item, etc. Include quotes from movers and anything else pertaining to moving. Having all of it in the same place will make the next days and months easier for you.
- Decide whether to hire movers or do it yourself (it's probably not a good idea to undertake a large move yourself for a variety of reasons). Be sure that if you do hire movers, to select a reputable company.

- Dispose of hazardous materials such as paint, cleaners, ammunition, propane tanks, oil for lamps, matches etc. Movers are not permitted transport these.
- Obtain three quotes in writing so you are comparing like services. Ask each moving company for the same information. It's easier to compare when you have documents in front of you.
- Take pictures of your furniture and electronics before packing so you have a record of their condition. While you're at it, write down the model and serial numbers of the electronics. Keep the photos and lists with your valuables (see below).
- As you're taking shelving and furniture apart, and pictures off the wall, place the screws, hangers and nails in a self-sealing plastic bag. Keep these in a tote bag you carry with you—preferably a brightly colored one so it's easily visible. Add the TV remote and any other small items that could be lost and will be needed quickly at your new home. Add a hammer, screwdriver, pliers, level.
- Obtain plenty of boxes, unprinted newspaper and bubble wrap.

    o   Boxes can either be bought or collected from stores willing to give them away. If you purchase boxes from your mover or other box suppliers, sometimes they are conveniently printed with room names on them.
        An average move will need a minimum of 100 boxes. Be prepared to get more if necessary. Remember that it's better to have more boxes well packed to prevent breakage than to have fewer boxes.

o Unprinted newspaper is cleaner to work with and will keep your precious items cleaner, as well. Ink from printed newspaper may stick permanently to dishes and most certainly make a mess of your hands. Call your local newspaper office and ask for end rolls. They are usually inexpensive and easy to work with. Paper can also be purchased from some moving companies and box suppliers.

o Bubble wrap is best for wrapping pictures, glass table tops and other large breakables. Be generous to ensure there's no breakage. Encase each wrapped item with cardboard for more protection. Affix "fragile" stickers.

- Popped popcorn is good, cheap and environmentally safe filler. Hold the butter and salt.
- Use only two or three sizes of boxes so movers can stack them safely. Tape the bottoms, as well as the tops, so they are secure.
- Use the best quality packing tape you can afford so it unrolls easily and does not split as you work. Using a tape dispenser makes this job easier.
- Pack an *Open Me First* box containing everything you will need for the first night in your new home, such as bedding, towels, tooth brush, toothpaste, drinking glass, toiletries, medications, pjs, coffee pot, mugs and coffee, paper plates, scissors, phone books, paper towels, bathroom tissue, cleanser, light bulbs, cleaning cloths, bottled water etc.
- Pack similar items together.
- Wrap pictures and mirrors in plenty of bubble wrap and secure.

- Wrap plates well and stand on their edges. Glasses, mugs and vases stand on their rims. Stuff plenty of paper inside, as well as around them, to prevent breakage.
- Fill boxes completely, using paper (towels, T-shirts and socks) if necessary to stuff the extra space, so there is no movement inside the box.
- Pack books, CDs, paper and anything else heavy in the bottom of the box with lighter items on top so the boxes don't become too heavy to lift. This is a good place to use pillows, towels, T-shirts, paper towels (on the roll) and the like as filler. Use smaller boxes for heavier items.
- Number the boxes as indicated in the Appendix to make unpacking much easier. Add more lines if necessary to have more space to list the box's contents.
- Write or stick a label on each box (every side and top) with the name of the destination room on it. If your boxes have room names printed on them, check off the appropriate name.
- Use "fragile" and "this side up" stickers when necessary. Point this out to the movers when they arrive. If you need to tape over the sticker to ensure it stays on the box, do so.
- Pack with care. Use more packing paper than you think you need to ensure nothing is broken. Better to have many well-packed boxes than fewer boxes in which your treasures might be damaged.
- Begin packing everything not in use. Think off-season clothing, decorations, sports equipment.
- Clothes can be left in dresser drawers.
- Use wardrobe boxes for clothes on hangers. These can usually be borrowed from your moving company. They

will bring the boxes on moving day to be filled and taken away once emptied.

- Add shoes, bedding, and towels (if not used as packing) in the bottom of wardrobe boxes.
- Keep valuables (jewelry, personal records, school info, medical and financial records, insurance info) with you. Included in this list is your Log containing all the data you need for your move.
- Back up software and data files. Keep computer backups with your valuables.
- Stack boxes in the room you use least. When stacking them, place heavier boxes on bottom.
- Stack same sizes of recycled boxes together so they do not break.
- Set a daily or weekly goal to pack a certain number of boxes.
- Arrange in advance for the movers to make crates for large pictures, glass table tops, mirrors.
- Movers can pack your computer, TV, antiques and large items. Ensure they have insurance in case of any damage and arrange for this in advance.
- If possible, arrange to have children and pets off site for the move.

The eagle has landed!!

- Unpack your *Open Me First* box.

- As soon as your beds are assembled, make them so they're ready for you to fall into when you're ready.
- Clean the bathroom first, including the shower.
- Clean the kitchen sink and counters so when you're ready to eat, they're ready as well.
- Take a break now and enjoy being in your new home. The rest can wait for tomorrow when you're refreshed.

Packing for a Senior

Be aware that some dementia may be present and the person may not understand why he or she needs to move. It's understandable that the individual may not believe it's necessary, and resist. You may find he or she unpacks behind your back as soon as you've completed a box if the understanding is fuzzy.

When packing for a senior, note that forgetful seniors tend to hide valuables and not remember they did so. During one senior move I was involved with, we found thousands of dollars in cash stashed away. Be sure to check every pocket, purse, container, book, cereal box etc. for valuables. Watch for jewelry too, as well as security certificates, bonds, safety deposit box keys and whatever else you can think of that fits your unique situation. Look in places that don't appear to be hiding places—you may be surprised at what you find.

While you're at it, you may find paperwork that may be used to steal identity. Keep this aside to deal with later—whether it's to be acted upon, filed or shredded.

Forgetful seniors may also not remember that they have given a particular item away and begin to believe it was stolen. Be prepared to help the senior be at peace with their decision.

I remember when Isobel, then in her early 90s, gave her kitchen set to a granddaughter. Some months later, she accused this granddaughter of stealing it. Of course, this resulted in much angst for the family.

Begin by identifying belongings going to their new place. Once the senior knows favorite items will go along, he or she may be more ready to let go of the rest. Be prepared to tell them, in detail, where every item has gone.

Be aware that they may want to take a piece or two of furniture that isn't suitable. Have your elder show you how to open a drawer if the dresser is not worth keeping or the drawers stick. This will help them understand they need to let it go. Ensure also that moved pieces are safe and not liable to break if any weight is applied.

If necessary, rent a storage locker and sort one box at a time after the move. Don't fall into the trap of keeping it longer than a few months or it will never be empty. The temptation is too strong to let things stay there and not deal with them.

IV WHAT'S NEXT?

"Knowing things will change can be exciting. There is a sense of adventure when we understand that there will be new challenges, that we will wake up each day not to the sameness of yesterday but to new experiences and new problem-solving opportunities."[1]

This is the time to focus on your new life and on activities you previously had no time for. A relative began drawing when she moved to a smaller home, and subsequently sold several of her pieces to her local public library. That she developed her artistic side was a pleasant surprise to her family.

You might find it enlightening to get to know yourself again. Or even reinvent yourself. Your new life may be less formal and more relaxed. Or you might find one or more volunteer activities that are enjoyable and helpful to others. This is also an opportunity to meet new friends.

Settling in

- Unpack carefully. You will have labeled all your boxes, so open the ones containing items you need first, and work through the rest according to what you need next. Some boxes may remain packed and put into storage, e.g. Christmas decorations or off-season clothing.
- Keep it simple.
- Plan a treat for yourself once you've settled—a trip, a day at the spa, a fishing trip, even a day just to relax and read.
- Invite family and/or friends for a meal. This is your new home and it's time to create new memories.
- You may find you need to wade through your belongings and purge again. (When I moved from a home I lived in for 18 years, I thought I'd got rid of everything that needed to go. Once in the new house, another large yard sale was undertaken, then another one a few years later.)
- If something doesn't resonate in a positive way in your new home, let it go.
- Enjoy the lightness and liberation you now feel in your new home.
- Enjoy learning who you are now, and who you are becoming in this new chapter of your life.

Celebrate your future

- More time to travel

- Less housework
- Work on hobbies
- Enjoy family and friends
- List all the things you ever wanted to do and begin fulfilling those dreams (think Bucket List)
- Stop living to have and start living to become. Create space to grow.

Food for thought: Have you ever seen a U-Haul following a hearse?

> "The great thing in this world is not so much where we stand,
> as in what direction we are moving."
> ~Oliver Wendall Holmes (1809-1894, Poet, Physician)

V ADVICE FROM THOSE WHO HAVE BEEN THERE

- Don't wait until circumstances force you to downsize. Start now.
- Make a plan.
- Keep the minimum necessary.
- Don't try to do it all alone. Ask someone you trust who can pull you back on track if you stray, or remind you why you're doing this.
- Ask for help both for motivation and organization. And maybe even for the heavy lifting.
- Do a bit every day; don't try to do it all the same day or you'll exhaust yourself and possibly abandon the project.
- If you have a partner, start early and try to be firm with that person if he/she is a saver.
- Once you've downsized, don't allow more stuff to accumulate. Space is finite and can hold only so much. For everything new coming in, something that takes the same amount of space must go.
- Think things through in advance, i.e. paperwork, life insurance etc.

- Prepare a list of your investments and where they are, the contact person, bank accounts and safety deposit box.
- Discuss everything, even through difficulties.
- Assign items to a recipient early if possible so there's no confusion later.
- Family cottage—who gets it? Better to discuss this when your parent is in better health. It's more difficult to get information when a parent degenerates. This will also avoid later misunderstandings.
- Whatever discussions and arrangements can be made in advance—make sure everyone concerned or potentially concerned knows about it. If parents make arrangements with one child and do not tell the others, that's a recipe for later disaster and possibly lawsuits.
- When gift shopping, choose consumables rather than tangible items unless the recipient has asked for something specific. Think of flowers, dinner out, your time, movie tickets, tickets to a show, museum, sports event, a trip or a drive in the country, manicure, pedicure, day at the spa etc. Let your imagination run wild here to see how many consumables you can think of.

AFTERWORD

When all is said and done, downsizing, moving and settling into your new place will have been a good experience—if you look at it with a positive attitude.

Yes, you probably had some ups and downs emotionally and physically, but you survived. And you have so much to look forward to. Life gives us gifts when we least expect them. Making space for new experiences and new relationships cannot help but create a forward-looking attitude.

Enjoy all that life has to offer. It's too short to dwell on negatives.

To everything there is a season.
A time to get and a time to lose.
A time to keep and a time to cast away.
~ Ecclesiastes 3:1, 6 [1] KJV

APPENDIX—SAMPLE PACKING LOG

Box Number	Contents
1	
2	
3	
4	

BIBLIOGRAPHY/ADDITIONAL READING

CULBERTSON, Judi and Decker, Marj, *Scaling Down, Living Large in a Smaller Space*, 2005, Rodale Inc. Publishers, USA.

DELLAQUILA, Vickie, *Don't Toss My Memories in the Trash, A Step-by-Step Guide to Helping Seniors Downsize, Organize and Move*, 2007, Mountain Publishing. Available from Organization Rules, Inc. 412-913-0554.

GIBSON, Katherine, *Unclutter Your Life: Transforming Your Physical, Mental and Emotional Space*, 2004, Beyond Words Publishing, Hillsboro, Oregon.

KUBLER-ROSS, Elizabeth, *On Death and Dying*, 1969, MacMillan Publishing Co., Inc., New York, New York.

LADD, Karol, *A Positive Plan for Creating More Calm, Less Stress*, 2005, W Publishing Group, Nashville, Tennessee.

MANNING, Doug, *When Love Gets Tough, The Nursing Home Decision*, 1983, In-Sight Books Inc., Hereford, Texas.

RHODES, Ann, *Guidance and Support in Caring for the Elderly*, 1989, Grosvenor House Press Inc., Montreal, Quebec.

SCHIFF, Harriet Sarnoff, *How Did I Become My Parent's Parent?*, 1996, Penguin Books Canada Ltd., Toronto, Ontario.

SCHLENGER, Sunny, *Organizing for the Spirit, Making the Details of Your Life Meaningful and Manageable*, 2004, Josey-Bass, A Wiley Imprint, San Francisco, California.

TABB, Mark, *Living with Less: the upside of downsizing your life*, 2006, Bordman & Holman Publishers, Nashville, Tennessee.

THOMAS, Kim, *Simplicity: Finding Peace by Uncluttering Your Life*, 1999, Broadman & Holman Publishers, Nashville, Tennessee.

WHATLEY, Alice, *Peaceful Spaces: Transform Your Home into a Haven of Calm and Tranquility*, 2002, Ryland Peters & Small Inc. New York, New York.

WEBSITES OF INTEREST:

At the time of publication, the following websites were active:

"Who Gets Grandma's Yellow Pie Plate?" University of Minnesota Extension Service:
http://www.yellowpieplate.umn.edu/

"Ultimate shelf life guide for food" Still Tasty LLC:
http://www.stilltasty.com/

Professional Organizers in Canada (POC)
http://www.organizersincanada.com

National Association for Professional Organizers (NAPO)
http://www.napo.net/

Institute for Challenging Disorganization
www.challengingdisorganization.org

Professional Organizer Association of Africa (POAA)
http://www.poaa.co.za/

Australasian Association of Professional Organizers Inc. (AAPO)
www.aapo.org.au

Association of Professional Declutterers and Organizers UK
(APDO-UK)
http://www.apdo-uk.co.uk/

ENDNOTES

Introduction:

[1] http://www.merriam-webster.com/

Chapter I

[1] http://www.wordspy.com/
[2] Peaceful Spaces p. 10
[3] Unclutter Your Life, p. 43
[4] http://www.yellowpieplate.umn.edu/indexB.html

Chapter II

[1] How Did I Become My Parent's Parent? P. 7

Chapter III

[1] How Did I Become My Parent's Parent? p. 68

Afterword

[1] The Holy Bible, King James Version